Yallas

BROTHER'S
KEEPER

Written and Compiled by
Rod Terry

Design by
Evelyn Loeb and
Arlene Greco

Words of Inspiration
for African-American Men

PETER PAUPER PRESS, INC.
WHITE PLAINS, NEW YORK

For Fred, Eursalean, "Termite," Dawanna,
DaShunda, and all of the brothers
in the struggle.

Photographs reprinted with the permission
of FPG International Corp.: Ron Rovtar
photo p. 6; Barry Rosenthal photo p. 12;
Ron Chapple photos pp. 19, 24, and 42;
Reggie Parker photo p. 30; Walter Smith
photo p. 36; Michael Goldman photo p. 39;
Diane Padys photo p. 48; and Mark Harmel
photo p. 56

Contents

INTRODUCTION

Within the pages of this little book are words of wisdom and inspirational thoughts that are intended to motivate, inspire, and nurture the actions of Black men everywhere. *Brother's Keeper: Words of Inspiration for African-American Men* represents the collective wisdom, hopes, visions, experiences, and thinking of many contemporary and historical Black men who have had a dramatic impact on the world. It includes the wisdom and wit of, among many others, Dr. Martin Luther King, Jr., Dr. Benjamin E. Mays, Malcolm X, Nelson Mandela, Rev. Jesse Jackson, Jr., Colin L. Powell, and Bill Cosby.

We hope that *Brother's Keeper* will serve as the impetus which ignites a new movement among African-American men toward self-realization, character building, and Black empowerment. The time is now. The Black man must rise from the ashes like the Phoenix. W. E. B. Du Bois' statement, "There is within this world no such force, as the force of a man determined to rise," resounds with truth and urgency.

Brother's Keeper contains many expressions that can generate a sense of connectedness with our rich African-American heritage. These words can prepare us to face the challenges ahead, boldly and defiantly, with the assurance of the wisdom of the ages. Let us not underestimate the power of words to enlarge the spirit and liberate the mind.

R. T.

COURAGE

Courage is the power of the mind to over-come fear. It is one of the most supreme virtues that a man can possess. In order for Black men to prosper and take our rightful places in society, we must have the courage to surmount our fears. We must resolve within ourselves to be courageous in our fight against racism, poverty, and all other social conditions that threaten our community. There are no limitations to the strength and intellect of a man who is able to break the chain of fear. The fearless man is able to control his destiny in life.

History provides many examples of coura-geous Black men who were able to resist the shackles of fear and overcome the challenges of their time. The problems and issues that confront us today are not new. There is no reason for us to be afraid. Others before us have already tested the waters and mastered their currents.

As African-American men, we need to be more daring in our approach to life. Life has much more to offer than the same daily routine of least resistance and complacency. We must dare to take risks, face the unknown, go against the odds. Courage gives us the strength to overcome in spite of obstacles set before us. We must also have the courage to question authority and not always blindly and passively submit to the pressures and dictates of the system. We must be self-possessed and, more than anything else, have the unyielding courage to stand alone.

✦ ✦ ✦ ✦ ✦ ✦ ✦ ✦ ✦

The ultimate measure of a man is not where he stands in moments of comfort and convenience, but where he stands at times of challenge and controversy.

DR. MARTIN LUTHER KING, JR.

I would rather go to hell by choice than to stumble into heaven by following the crowd.

DR. BENJAMIN E. MAYS

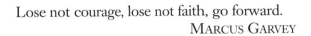

Lose not courage, lose not faith, go forward.
MARCUS GARVEY

Never let your head hang down. Never give up and sit and grieve. Find another way. And don't pray when it rains if you don't pray when the sun shines.
SATCHEL PAIGE

It's never the right time to take a particular stand.
ADAM CLAYTON POWELL, JR.

The free man is the man with no fears.
DICK GREGORY

It takes no courage to get in the back of a crowd and throw a rock.
THURGOOD MARSHALL

The hallmark of courage in this age of conformity is to stand up for what you believe.

CURTLAND MILLOY

We must constantly build dikes of courage to hold back the flood of tears.

DR. MARTIN LUTHER KING, JR.

Waiting is a window opening on many landscapes. . . . To continue one's journey in the darkness with one's footsteps guided by the illumination of remembered radiance is to know courage of a peculiar kind—the courage to demand that light continue to be light even in the surrounding darkness. To walk in the light while darkness invades, envelops, and surrounds is to wait on the Lord. This is to know the renewal of strength. This is to walk and faint not.

HOWARD THURMAN

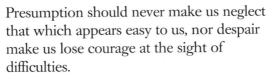

Presumption should never make us neglect
that which appears easy to us, nor despair
make us lose courage at the sight of
difficulties.

BENJAMIN BANNEKER

I believe . . . that living on the edge, living in
and through your fear, is the summit of life,
and that people who refuse to take that dare
condemn themselves to a life of living death.

JOHN H. JOHNSON

The guy who takes a chance, who walks the
line between the known and unknown, who is
unafraid of failure, will succeed.

GORDON PARKS

Fear is an illusion.

MICHAEL JORDAN

SENSE OF PURPOSE

A well-defined sense of purpose provides a road map that guides and directs our journey through life. Life is simpler and more meaningful when we set goals for ourselves and have a particular mission in mind. Goals propel us into action and give us the driving force necessary to face life's challenges. More simply stated, goals give us a reason to get up in the morning. Even if we occasionally diverge from our path, our sense of purpose helps us to stay on a charted course.

Nelson Mandela, President of South Africa, is the best modern-day example of living with a purpose. Despite 27 years of imprisonment and the daunting challenges that faced him, he never lost sight of his vision to free South Africa from the shackles of apartheid.

Life offers infinite possibilities. We must each choose our individual path in life. Our major task is to define who we are and who we will

become. Do not assume a restricted
or provincial place in this world. There is an
urgency in our community that obliges us to
take charge of our lives.

✦ ✦ ✦ ✦ ✦ ✦ ✦ ✦

If you haven't dreamed that you will get there,
you will not think about ever taking the steps
to be there.

MAX ROBINSON

The man who simply sets and waits
    Fur good to come along,
Ain't worth the breath that one would take
    To tell him he is wrong.
Fur good ain't flowin' round this world
    Fur every fool to sup;
You've got to put your see-ers on,
    An' go an' hunt it up.

PAUL LAURENCE DUNBAR,
My Sort o' Man

Along with enthusiasm, dedication and persistence, you've got to be realistic.

ARTHUR ASHE

Life takes on meaning when you become motivated, set goals, and charge after them in an unstoppable manner.

LES BROWN

Strive to make something of yourselves; then strive to make the most of yourselves.

ALEXANDER CRUMMEL

We need to dream big dreams, propose grandiose means if we are to recapture the excitement, the vibrancy, and pride we once had.

COLEMAN YOUNG

Persistence and positive attitude are necessary ingredients for any successful venture.

L. DOUGLASS WILDER

There is in this world no such force as the force of a man determined to rise. The human soul cannot be permanently chained.

W. E. B. DU BOIS

To be who you are and become what you are capable of is the only goal worth living.

ALVIN AILEY

If you expect somebody else to guide you, you'll be lost.

JAMES EARL JONES

The major threat to blacks in America has not been oppression, but rather the loss of hope and absence of meaning.

CORNEL WEST

Even if I wanted to forget the fact that I was black as a child, there were always people who would not let me forget. I didn't have hate for the way people made differences known. It just toughened me up. It just made me want to beat them in everything. It made me want to be superior in everything.

MICHAEL HUYGHUE

A man who stands for nothing will fall for anything.

MALCOLM X

Whether or not you reach your goals in life depends entirely on how well you prepare for them and how badly you want them. . . . You're eagles! Stretch your wings and fly to the sky!

RONALD MCNAIR

Take advantage of every opportunity; where there is none, make it for yourself.

MARCUS GARVEY

In life you are as small as your controlling desire or as great as your dominant aspiration.

ARMSTRONG WILLIAMS

Mix a conviction with a man and something happens.

ADAM CLAYTON POWELL, JR.

There is something in every one of you that waits and listens for the sound of the genuine in yourself. It is the only true guide you will ever have. And if you cannot hear it, you will all of your life spend your days on the ends of strings that somebody else pulls.

HOWARD THURMAN

Never give up. Keep your thoughts and your mind always on the goal.

TOM BRADLEY

BROTHERHOOD

In years past it was an expected and accepted social norm that Black people looked out for each other. We could leave our doors unlocked and be assured that the neighbor across the street would keep a watchful eye until we returned. There was an understanding within the community that if one of the neighborhood children "showed-out" down the street, while out of sight of his parents, he could be disciplined by *any* adult member of the community. There was a true sense of "love they neighbor." Backslapping and altruism were the order of the day. This sort of caretaking unified the Black community and held us together.

Our success depends on our ability to recapture that sense of community. "We must learn to live together as brothers. Or we will perish together as fools," counseled Dr. Martin Luther King, Jr. The old adage remains true: "There is strength in unity."

Black men in particular must strive to form stronger bonds with each other. Embracing and supporting our brothers does not compromise our masculinity. We must develop among ourselves a greater feeling of solidarity, kinship, and brotherhood. This is the surest means by which we can transform our communities into the protective and nurturing havens they once were.

✦ ✦ ✦ ✦ ✦ ✦ ✦ ✦ ✦

A man has to act like a brother before you can call him a brother.

MALCOLM X

As you seek your way in the world, never fail to find a way to serve your community. Use your education and your success in life to help those still trapped in cycles of poverty and violence.

COLIN L. POWELL

There is an African proverb which succinctly captures the humanity upon which a sense of community is founded:

Umuntu ngumuntu ngabanye ngabantu
Motho ke motho ka batho

The broad meaning of this proverb is that each person's humanity is ideally expressed through his or her relationship with others, and theirs in turn, through a recognition of that person's humanity.

NELSON MANDELA

A sure way for someone to lift himself up is by helping to lift someone else.

BOOKER T. WASHINGTON

We have the right and, above all, we have the duty to bring strength and support of our entire community to defend the lives and property of each individual family.

PAUL ROBESON

We are inevitably our brother's keeper
because we are our brother's brother.
Whatever affects one directly affects all
indirectly.

DR. MARTIN LUTHER KING, JR.

America's massive social breakdown requires
that we come together–for the sake of our
lives, our children, and our sacred honor.

CORNEL WEST

SELF-ESTEEM

A sense of self-worth is critical to our happiness and success in life. Self-esteem is part of the nuts and bolts that make us strong Black men. How we are perceived by others mirrors how we feel about ourselves. Muhammad Ali, former heavyweight boxing champion, counsels, "To be a great champion you must believe you are the best. If you're not, pretend you are."

A positive self-image is also a starting point for building and maintaining strong relationships with others. When we love and respect ourselves, we are able to share these same feelings with others and establish more meaningful relationships.

How do we build self-esteem? Only through deliberate and serious introspection are we able to develop a positive self-concept. Self-esteem is raised when we acknowledge and take pride in our achievements, make accurate and honest assessments of our strengths and weaknesses, and learn to recognize and appreciate our own attributes and talents.

Black men should be especially conscious that negative thoughts and images undermine self-esteem more than any other factors. Our thoughts have the power to make us or to break us. How we feel about ourselves is more important than how others portray us. What really matters is our own interpretation of who we are. Self-confidence and assurance are states of mind that all of us can project.

✦ ✦ ✦ ✦ ✦ ✦ ✦ ✦

If you have no confidence in self, you are twice defeated in the race of life. With confidence, you have won even before you have started.

MARCUS GARVEY

We have to *think* positively about ourselves. We must *believe* that we can overcome any obstacle. Face any fault. Climb any mountain. Cross any river. Believe we can turn the impossible into the possible, the unbearable into the bearable and the unbelievable into the believable.

MARION BARRY

The Black artist. The Black man. The holy man. The man you seek. The climber, the striver. The maker of peace. The lover. The warrior. We are they whom you seek. Look in. Find yourself. Find the being, the speaker.

IMAMU AMIRI BARAKA

The collapse of character begins with compromise.

FREDERICK DOUGLASS

You have to know you can win. You have to think you can win. You *feel* you can win. . . . Call it a plus.

SUGAR RAY LEONARD

I think one of my basic flaws has been a lack of esteem . . . always feeling like I had to do more. I never could do enough or be good enough.

MAX ROBINSON

The most important thing I have to fight as a black person in an oppressive, racist society is what I think about myself.

MARK MATHABANE

I did not equate my self-worth with my wins and losses.

ARTHUR ASHE

Lack of self-confidence and the fear of failure are opposite sides of the same coin.

CHARLES B. JOHNSON

With a spirit straining toward true self-esteem, the Negro must boldly throw off the manacles of self-abnegation and say to himself and the world: "I am somebody. I am a person. I am a man with dignity and honor. I have a rich and noble history."

DR. MARTIN LUTHER KING, JR.

Rise, Brothers! Come let us possess this land. Never say: "Let well enough alone." Cease to console yourselves with adages that numb the moral sense. Be discontented. . . . Let your discontent break mountain-high against the wall of prejudice, and swamp it to the very foundation. Then we shall not have to plead for justice nor on bended knee crave mercy; for we shall be men.

JOHN HOPE

If it falls your lot to be a street sweeper, sweep streets as Raphael painted pictures, sweep streets as Michelangelo carved marble, sweep streets as Beethoven composed music, or Shakespeare wrote poetry.

DR. MARTIN LUTHER KING, JR.

If you respect yourself, it's easier to respect other people.

JOHN SINGLETON

EDUCATION

Some of the most inspiring words that I have ever heard came from a college professor, Dr. Addie Mitchell, when I was a freshman at Morehouse College. In her address to incoming freshmen during orientation week, Dr. Mitchell stated:

> *If you plan for a year, sow a seed;*
> *If you plan for a decade, plant a tree;*
> *If you plan for a century,* educate *the people.*

This thought-provoking statement has always remained with me, and has helped me to appreciate the far-reaching value and significance of a good education. Education is a ladder. It allows us to climb to new and unforeseen heights.

The future of the African-American community depends on the quality of our education. We should always be involved in the quest for knowledge. Education liberates our minds and widens our horizons, and it gives us the ability to make more informed choices.

Education is by far the most conventional means of opening doors of opportunity. A good education, however, goes beyond obtaining a college degree, or learning a vocational trade and landing a good job. The pursuit of education is an ongoing process. We live in an ever-changing world which requires us constantly to be prepared to adapt to new ideas, different cultures, and conflicting views.

❖ ❖ ❖ ❖ ❖ ❖ ❖ ❖ ❖

The paradox of education is precisely this— that as one begins to become conscious, one begins to examine the society in which he is being educated.

JAMES BALDWIN

Education is the primary tool of emancipation and liberation for African-Americans in our fight for true equality in this country.

EARL G. GRAVES

A good head and a good heart are always a formidable combination.

NELSON MANDELA

Nothing is more important than a good education.

ROY WILKINS

When we go into action and confront our adversaries, we must be as armed with knowledge as they.

DR. MARTIN LUTHER KING, JR.

My contemplation of life . . . taught me that he who cannot change the very fabric of his thought . . . will never be able to change reality, and will never, therefore, make any progress.

ANWAR SADAT

O my body, make of me always a man who questions!

FRANTZ FANON

Education is your passport to the future, for tomorrow belongs to the people who prepare for it today.

MALCOLM X

Real knowledge, properly used, will help anyone.

ROMARE BEARDEN

Always know that there is unlimited power in a developed mind and a disciplined spirit. If your mind can conceive it and your heart can believe it, you can achieve it. Suffering breeds character; character breeds faith, and in the end faith will prevail.

REV. JESSE L. JACKSON, JR.

We cannot afford to settle for being just average; we must learn as much as we can to be the best that we can. The key word is *education*–that's knowledge–education with maximum effort.

BILL COSBY

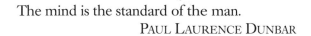

The mind is the standard of the man.
PAUL LAURENCE DUNBAR

We have not yet made education a process
whereby students are taught to respect the
inalienable dignity of other human beings.
DR. KENNETH B. CLARK

Without education you are not going
anywhere in this world.
MALCOLM X

If I had my magic wand and I were addressing
all Blacks . . . I would say there is no substitute
for hard work and education.
MERVYN DYMALLY

Nothing pains some people more than having
to think.
DR. MARTIN LUTHER KING, JR

SPIRITUALITY

Spirituality is the link between human beings and God. It connects us to the divine forces of the universe and helps us to realize the true essence of our being and meaning in life. In Biblical terms, faith is the substance of things hoped for, the evidence of things not seen. It is through *spirituality* and *faith* in the divine that we are able to conquer our fears and overcome our burdens.

By nature, we are a spiritual people. We are connected to a glorious African spiritual culture. As Black men, we must reclaim our ancestral powers and embrace our spirituality.

Spiritual growth requires meditation and nurturing. To tap into your spiritual self, be still. Learn to listen to yourself, and to follow your inner voice. When we are confronted with problems and hardships in life, we have a tendency to look to outside sources for guidance. However, we should recognize that solutions to day-to-day trials can be found within ourselves. We must seek our own counsel rather than always seeking the advice of others. God gives us the serenity of spirit to change our own circumstances.

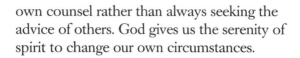

I am convinced that the universe is under the control of a loving purpose, and that in the struggle for righteousness man has cosmic companionship. Behind the harsh appearance of the world there is a benign power.
DR. MARTIN LUTHER KING, JR.

The greatest riches of our community are not material but moral.
DAVID N. DINKINS

It is our duty to conserve our physical powers, our intellectual endowments, our spiritual ideals.
W. E. B. DU BOIS

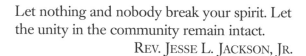

Let nothing and nobody break your spirit. Let the unity in the community remain intact.

REV. JESSE L. JACKSON, JR.

Our faith must be sustained by our passion for dignity and our trust in God . . .

ADAM CLAYTON POWELL, JR.

You can't regiment spirit, and it is the spirit that counts.

ROMARE BEARDEN

America has abandoned the strong woman of spirituality and is shacking up with the harlot of materialism.

JOSEPH LOWERY

Man is a being of spirit.

DR. MARTIN LUTHER KING, JR.

All human beings are periodically tested by the power of the universe. . . . how one performs under pressure is the true measure of one's spirit, heart, and desire.

SPIKE LEE

Lift up yourselves . . . take yourselves out of the mire and hitch your hopes to the stars.

FREDERICK DOUGLASS

Only through an inner spiritual transformation do we gain the strength to fight vigorously the evils of the world in a humble and loving spirit.

DR. MARTIN LUTHER KING, JR.

Death is not the end for someone who has faith.

BISHOP DESMOND TUTU

BLACK PRIDE

The Black Power movement, which evolved from the 1960s Civil Rights struggle, was one of the most positive periods in African-American history. During this period, Black people proudly acknowledged and celebrated their Black heritage. The desire to assimilate into the larger European culture, as had been the tradition, was substantially minimized. Dashikis, Afros, and clenched fists became symbolic images of Black Pride. Black people felt good about being Black. James Brown's hit song, "Say It Loud, I'm Black and I'm Proud," truly captured the mood of this era.

We should use this period as a model for rediscovering ourselves and the beauty of our African-American heritage. Despite the injustices we have all endured, and continue to endure, because of the color of our skin, there is an insurmountable joy in being Black. Black nationalist Marcus Garvey declared, "I would be nothing else in God's creation but a Black man."

Each of us should strive to capture the same sense of black pride that inspired two Black athletes, Tommie Smith and John Carlos, to raise their fists in the Black Power salute when they received winning medals at the 1968 Summer Olympic Games in Mexico City. Their message was clear and timeless– "Black is beautiful."

❖ ❖ ❖ ❖ ❖ ❖ ❖ ❖ ❖

Lift up your head, you mighty race!

MARCUS GARVEY

I have never been able to discover that there was anything disgraceful in being a colored man.

BERT WILLIAMS

We build our temples for tomorrow, strong as we know how, and we stand on top of the mountain, free within ourselves.

LANGSTON HUGHES

We ourselves have to lift the level of our community, the standard of our community to a higher level, make our own society beautiful so that we will be satisfied. We've got to change our minds about each other.

MALCOLM X

It is impossible to love ourselves without having an affection for Africa.

RANDALL ROBINSON

Let us hold up our heads and with firm and steady tread go manfully forward.

BOOKER T. WASHINGTON

Our Black heritage must be a foundation stone we can build on, not a place to withdraw to.

COLIN L. POWELL

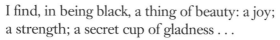

I find, in being black, a thing of beauty: a joy;
a strength; a secret cup of gladness . . .

OSSIE DAVIS

We will not stop until the heavy weight of
centuries of oppression is removed from our
backs and like proud men everywhere we can
stand tall together again.

JAMES FARMER

We must give our children a sense of pride in
being Black. The glory of our past and the
dignity of our present must lead the way to
the power of our future.

ADAM CLAYTON POWELL, JR.

I can move between different disciplines
because I am essentially a storyteller, and the
story I want to tell is about black people. I
always want to share my great satisfaction at
being a black man at this time in history.

OSSIE DAVIS

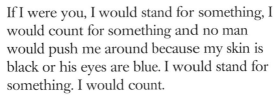

If I were you, I would stand for something, I would count for something and no man would push me around because my skin is black or his eyes are blue. I would stand for something. I would count.

DR. BENJAMIN E. MAYS

Black consciousness is the realization by the black man of the need to rally together with his brothers. It seeks to infuse the black community with a new-found pride.

STEVEN BIKO

We shall have our manhood.

ELDRIDGE CLEAVER

that will nourish your mind and soul as you contemplate what it takes to be a courageous Black man.

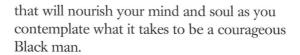

Create, and be true to yourself, and depend only on your own good taste.

DUKE ELLINGTON

Thinking your way through your problem is better than wishing your way through.

COLEMAN YOUNG

Failure is a word that I simply don't accept. As long as you don't accept it, you're not failing.

JOHN H. JOHNSON

If you know what you want, you will recognize it when you see it.

BILL COSBY

Do a common thing in an uncommon way.

BOOKER T. WASHINGTON

Dream big dreams! Others may deprive you of your material wealth and cheat you in a thousand ways, but no man can deprive you of the control and use of your imagination.

REV. JESSE L. JACKSON, JR.

You must not measure a man by the heights he has reached, but by the depths from which he has come.

FREDERICK DOUGLASS

Do not ever let others define you, or limit you,
or tell you what you believe.

RONALD H. BROWN

My father dreamed of the day when his son
would work in a towering office with a city
view. What he didn't know was that arriving
there would not be the end of the struggle for
black Americans.

LAWRENCE OTIS GRAHAM

Judge not thy brother!
There are secrets in his heart that you might
weep to see.

EGBERT MARTIN

The secret to success is to learn to accept the
impossible, to do without the indispensable,
and to bear the intolerable.

NELSON MANDELA

There is nothing more tragic than to find an individual bogged down in the length of life, devoid of the breadth.

DR. MARTIN LUTHER KING, JR.

You have to look at reality. . . . Once you cloud your vision with sentimentality, you are in trouble.

COLEMAN YOUNG

You've got to get the mind cleared out before you put the truth in it.

MINISTER LOUIS FARRAKHAN

Align yourself with powerful people. Align yourself with people that you can learn from, people who want more out of life, people who are stretching and searching and seeking some higher ground in life.

LES BROWN

We are responsible for the world in which we find ourselves, if only because we are the only sentient force which can change it.

JAMES BALDWIN

Success is the result of perfection, hard work, learning from failure, loyalty, and persistence.

COLIN L. POWELL

A person completely wrapped up in himself makes a small package.

DENZEL WASHINGTON

Learn to speak kind words. Nobody resents them.

CARL ROWAN

You never know which key unlocks the safe.

BRYANT GUMBEL

Life is not about what you get. Life is about what you do.

KURT L. SCHMOKE

Truth is proper and beautiful in all times and in all places.

FREDERICK DOUGLASS

The millenium approaches. We are about to turn the corner on the 21st century. Our prosperity is not guaranteed. Our freedom and our survival are not guaranteed.

AUGUST WILSON

BIOGRAPHICAL INDEX